BENEATH THE SURFACE

30 WAYS TO PRAY FOR JAPAN

1
2
3
4 **Ancestor veneration**
5 **Harmony**
6 **Social conformity**
7 **Self-reliance and materialism**
8 **Mental and emotional health**
9 **Aging society**
10 **Politics and international relations**
11 **Immigration and foreign nationals**
12 **Natural disasters**
13 **Technology and media**
14 **Workplace pressure**
15 **Family life**
16 **Youth and young adults**
17 **Struggling churches**
18 **Church planting**
19 **Church leadership**
20 **Church in the community**
21 **Creative ways of ministry**
22 **Christianity in rural areas**
23 **Personal evangelism**
24 **Faith in the workplace**
25 **Daily Christian life and faith**
26 **Japanese overseas**
27 **Missionary life**
28 **Unity in Christ**
29 **Japanese mission movement**
30 **Prayer for spiritual breakthrough**

Japan is a G7 country and is known as one of the biggest economies in Asia. It has been about 500 years since Christianity first came to Japan, but Christians are still a small minority among many religious groups (mostly Buddhist and Shinto). Over the years, many missionaries have preached the gospel in Japan with their sweat and tears.

One of the fruits of those many years of tears and ministry is this prayer booklet published by OMF. In my opinion, there is no better timing for this booklet. Japan truly needs your prayers. I would like to express my gratitude and urge you to pray for Japan so that our country might turn back to the Lord Jesus Christ.

Toshinori Ishida
Board Chairman
Japan Evangelical Association (JEA)

For many decades, missionaries and Japanese believers have worked laboriously to share the gospel in Japan, and from a human perspective, seem to be making very limited headway. This prayer booklet is perhaps one of the most unifying tools we have seen in order to help us battle on the frontlines of the spiritual war waging in Japan.

Due to globalization, we have more access to each other, the body of Christ. We can pray in greater numbers and in greater unison. Will you pray together with us? We are praying for a spiritual awakening so great that it can only be attributed to the power of a loving, saving God who genuinely desires Japan for his own.

Nathan Snow
President
Japan Evangelical Missionary Association (JEMA)

From the editors

Japan is known for its natural beauty, distinctive culture, and advanced technology; there is much to admire. Visitors to Japan comment that people are considerate, streets are clean, trains are on time, food is presented beautifully. It is a land that leaves memorable first impressions.

But beneath the surface, there is so much more—more to admire, but also much to wrestle with. In this booklet, we invite you to move beyond those first impressions to engage with the stories and concerns of Christians in Japan. It is these concerns, and the knowledge that fewer than 1% of Japanese people know Jesus, that have led OMF and Pioneers to produce this prayer booklet.

From the outset, this has been a collaboration involving the contributions and help of many missionaries and Japanese Christians. Their insights and advice have been invaluable.

At the time of publishing, the long-term effects of the COVID-19 pandemic are as yet unknown and may impact some of the trends and data mentioned.

Please join us in praying for a breakthrough of the Holy Spirit in this nation we love. The topics in this booklet are big, but we know that God will hear and answer our prayers for his glory.

Lorna Ferguson, Wendy Marshall, Sarah Chang
Editorial team

And this is the confidence that we have toward him, that if we ask anything according to his will he hears us. And if we know that he hears us in whatever we ask, we know that we have the requests that we have asked of him.

1 John 5:14-15 (ESV)

Special thanks

Contributors

Levi Booth
Grant Buchholtz
Sarah Chang
Tim Cole
Matthew Cummings
Peter Dallman
John Edwards
Dan Ellrick
Ana Gamez
Ruth-Mae Ghent
Bruce Harris
John Houlette
Rosanne Jones
Tammy and Jon Junker
David Lewis
Roger W. Lowther
John Mehn
John Newton Webb
Simon Pleasants
Koyuki Sami
Stephanie Schatz
Darcy and Art Staddon
Atsuko Tateishi
Brian Tom
Hisho Uga
Dale Viljoen
Carlton Walker
Michael Widmer
Jonathan Wilson
Christina Winrich
Yoichi Yamaguchi

Designer

John Ruffin

Researcher

Megumi Kato

List of organizations that contributors work with: OMF International (Japan), Pioneers Japan, The Antioch Partners, Asian Access, Converge Worldwide, Evangelical Covenant Church, Grace Christian Fellowship, International Ministerial Fellowship, Japan Baptist Mission, Japan Council of Philippine Churches, Japan Evangelical Missionary Association (JEMA), Japan Presbyterian Mission (Mission to the World), OneHope Japan, SEND International, The Evangelical Alliance Mission (TEAM), Tokyo Christian University, and Worldwide Evangelization for Christ International Japan (WEC).

About Japan

126th emperor is Naruhito (since 2019)

Nihon or **Nippon** is the country's name in Japanese

18 cities and **524** towns are without a church[1]

3rd largest economy in the world

Main religions are **Shinto** and **Buddhism**

1 out of **8** Protestant churches have no pastor

127.1 million population

Tokyo is the most populated metropolis in the world

<1% of the population are Christians

Brief Christian history in Japan

1549 Jesuit missionary Francis Xavier arrives and growth follows

1587 Foreign missionaries banned

1614 Government ban on Christianity, widespread persecution of Christians until 1640

1639 Japan enters long period of national isolation

1853 US Commodore Matthew Perry demands that Japan opens its ports

1859 Protestant missionaries arrive

1873 Government ban of Christianity lifted

1870s Missionaries produce Japanese translations of the Bible

1941 Government orders Protestant denominations to merge

1947 Religious freedom guaranteed by post-war constitution

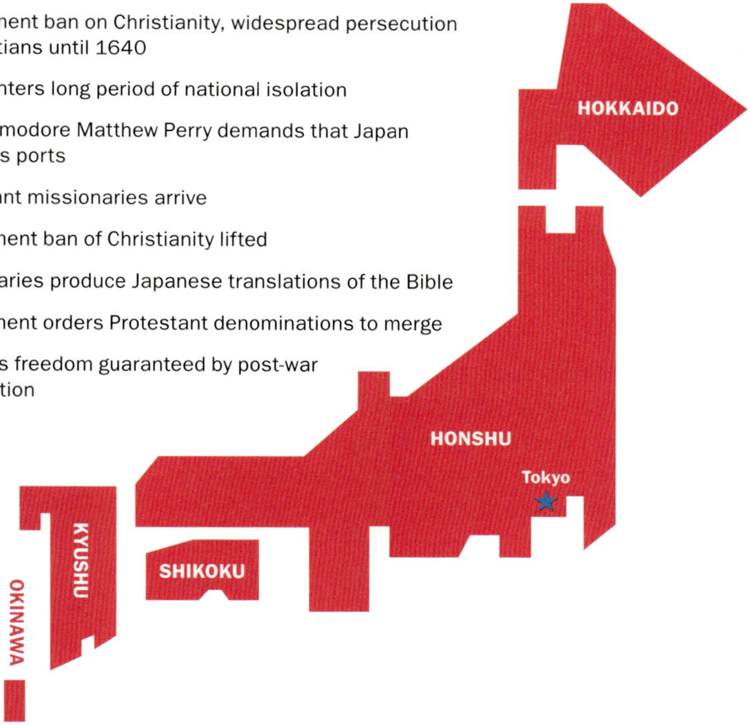

1

Popular religious practices

"Can I ask what you believe in?" Carlos* asked his Japanese friend Takeshi after watching him pray at the Shinto shrine.

"It's hard to explain," Takeshi replied slowly. "It's been part of my life since I was young."

Japanese people have gone to Shinto shrines and Buddhist temples for centuries. Many find comfort in repeating the simple rituals of purification and prayer. Faith or belief is not a prerequisite and anyone is welcome to join in. Such religious practices are deeply rooted in what it means to be Japanese.

At busy times, lines of people take turns to pray. They clap their hands and bow at the appropriate places. They buy charms to protect themselves from bad luck or to bring in good luck. They seek blessing for important life events, enjoy festivals, or find refreshment in the nature that is part of many religious sites.

Shrines and temples can be found in nearly every community in Japan, and many Japanese people view them as familiar places of belonging. Shinto and Buddhist influences have shaped Japanese society and identity in significant ways. But through Christ, Japanese people can find their deepest belonging in the God who created them.

*All names used in this booklet are pseudonyms.

Pray for wisdom to share the gospel within this Japanese context.

Pray that the Holy Spirit would lead those who seek salvation through various rituals to find Jesus Christ.

Pray that Japanese people would find their most authentic belonging and identity in the God who created them.

祈願
櫻井神社

2

Japanese views of Christianity

When Masako, a Japanese non-Christian lady, visited a church, she asked a church member about the meaning of a verse in a hymn. No one, not even the Bible school student, knew. The pastor only knew because he'd studied classical Japanese.

Due to experiences like Masako's, some Japanese people have an impression that Christianity is difficult to understand or is old-fashioned. Stereotypes can remain despite churches using modern Bible translations and songs. Other people may not know enough to have any opinion at all.

Further misunderstandings can emerge through contacts with Jehovah's Witnesses or cults that seem Christian. Without knowing the differences, people can turn away from seeking Jesus altogether.

Some people are deterred by the idea that Christianity is "Western" or foreign, although this aspect can attract others.

There are positive impressions too. Some Japanese people see Christians as caring or kind, involved with helping the poor or disadvantaged. Others see the Bible as a source of wisdom, or consult Christians whom they respect for advice. Despite being a tiny percentage of the population, many Christians have had a positive influence on society. Over the decades, they've started medical and educational institutions and, in recent years, responded to disasters.

Give thanks that many Christians are respected, and pray for open hearts toward Christ through them.

Pray that negative stereotypes or false ideas about Christianity will be changed through positive interactions with Christians.

Pray that Christians and churches would be welcoming and share the gospel in ways that are easy to understand.

3

Japanese culture and Christianity

Broken pottery pieces in Japan, instead of being thrown away, can be put back together with gold resin. This is an art called *kintsugi*. Experts tell us that there are eleven different ways an item of pottery can break. A *kintsugi* artisan is able to distinguish between them and knows how to bring beauty out of each one.

A Christian Japanese artist once described God as the master *kintsugi* artist. God searches for the brokenness in our lives and has the power to bring beauty out of it. There are many redemptive analogies in Japanese culture that point to God and can be used to help explain the gospel.[2]

However, for many Japanese believers, culture often feels like something that pulls them away from God rather than pointing to him, or is just confusing to think about. Shrines and temples feature in festivals and holidays, significant life events, and school field trips. On Sundays children and adults have to choose between church and mandatory sports practices or company outings. Some Christians face conflict within their families regarding religious traditions and expectations, such as ancestor veneration. Godly discernment is needed on a daily basis.

Pray that Japanese Christians would see God's redemptive analogies in their culture and use them to point people to Christ.

Pray that Japanese believers would have wisdom to make God-honoring decisions in their daily lives.

Pray that God would raise up more Japanese Christian artists to impact the culture in creative ways for his glory.

4

Ancestor veneration

Mrs. Sato knelt in front of the *butsudan*, the Buddhist altar in her home. She lit incense, struck a bell, and prayed for her family. Then she turned toward her deceased mother's photo to tell her about the grandchildren. Family altars have traditionally been the center of religious ritual within Japanese homes.

Japanese people's relationship to their ancestors is complex and varied. Many want to express gratitude and respect, or commune with loved ones. They ask their ancestors for help, or pray for their ancestors' souls. The relationship is usually understood to be reciprocal: the living take care of the dead and the dead take care of the living.

Some Japanese people believe that *butsudan* and grave rituals are sacred, but for others, social aspects outweigh religious ones. For example, a Japanese pastor explains that his mother placing a cup of coffee before a photo of her deceased husband is primarily an expression of grief. Christians need to distinguish between social and religious elements.

Many seekers want to know where deceased family members are. It is important for churches to address difficult questions well and to find appropriate biblical ways to show respect for ancestors.

Pray for wisdom and compassion for pastors as they answer seekers' questions.

Pray for freedom and peace in Christ for those who feel bound by fear or obligation to their ancestors.

Pray for Christians to find appropriate ways to remember those who have died and to care for their graves.

5

Harmony

"My daughter turned three last month," Aiko, a young Christian mother, explained to the missionary. "My mother-in-law wants the Shinto priest to pray for her at the *Shichi-Go-San* festival."*

The grandmother had argued that this was an important tradition and the first chance for the little girl to dress up in a formal *kimono*.

Aiko said, "If I refuse, she will say that I am ruining the harmony of the family."

As the missionary talked and prayed with Aiko, he realized that the grandmother just wanted the little girl to have a celebration. They decided to have a time of prayer for the children at church and encourage them to wear *kimonos*.

The grandmother came and took many photos; the little girl looked magnificent in her red-and-gold *kimono*. Parents were happy to have their children prayed for. A new church tradition had begun.

Harmony is a beautiful value in Japanese culture and arts, but it can have a darker side. People may avoid telling the truth if it ruins the harmony of the group. They may find it easier to avoid someone they disagree with rather than confront the issue. Students might not speak out when bullied, nor employees when their boss is wrong.

**Shichi-Go-San* is a Japanese festival to celebrate children's growth at seven, five, and three years old.

Give thanks for the love of harmony and pray it would be balanced with love of God's truth.

Pray for Japanese churches and Christians to find ways to live harmoniously with non-believers without compromising their faith.

Pray for wisdom and courage when Christians need to prioritize obedience to God over harmony.

6

Social conformity

"I could never become a Christian; no one in my family has ever been one. I would betray them if I did."

"My boss calls at 6 a.m. on my day off to tell me to come to work, so I have to go."

"I've never spoken about Jesus at work because I don't want to break the harmony."

"I don't want to pray at church because I can't pray like other people."

Pressure—to conform, to not make mistakes, to not admit weaknesses, to work beyond their limits—is often felt deeply by Japanese people. Many hide their true selves and are sensitive to how they are being viewed by others. When the daily stresses add up, the effects can be dire: mental health concerns, alcoholism, estranged families, and even suicide.

In a country where Christians are a tiny minority, pressure to conform can be felt as pressure not to become a Christian. For believers, conformity can be felt as pressure to keep their faith private and their struggles hidden.

In Christ, we find grace, acceptance, and rest, but in a pressurized society, those truths can be hard to believe and even harder to live out.

Give thanks for
Japanese believers who know that, through Jesus, God accepts them as they are.

Pray for Japanese people who are facing severe effects of stress to put their faith in Christ and receive his grace.

Pray that Japanese Christians would have wisdom from God to respond to social pressures.

7

Self-reliance and materialism

There are two words you're guaranteed to learn if you live in Japan:

Ganbatte—Do your best, keep going.

Shōganai—It can't be helped, there's nothing we can do.

Together these words demonstrate the spirit of self-reliance that is common in Japanese thinking. Most problems can be solved by simply trying harder. And the things that can't be solved this way are seen as things that just need to be tolerated.

People work long hours to provide financial security for their families. Students study late into the night in order to pass entrance exams. They are relying on themselves to "do their best."

In many ways this strong work ethic and determined perseverance is admirable. But without reliance on the merciful God who calls us to rest in him, it can lead to bitterness, burnout, and breakdowns—of individuals, families, and society.

Many Japanese apartments are filled with hard-earned comforts, but are empty of grace-filled relationships that give rest to the soul. And even missionaries need to keep a close watch on their hearts, that they don't end up preaching at themselves "*ganbatte*!" and "*shōganai*!" rather than resting in the Lord and relying on his help.

Pray for Japanese Christians and missionaries to demonstrate joyful dependency on God.

Pray for Japanese non-believers to see their limitations and need for God's grace.

Pray for grace and salvation to become as prevalent in Japan as *ganbatte* and *shōganai*.

8

Mental and emotional health

A missionary couple hosted Riku for four months at their home. For two years before then, he had shut himself inside his house, but had eventually been kicked out for being violent.

Riku was one of over a million people in Japan with *hikikomori*, a condition in which individuals shut themselves off from society for at least six months.[3] Yet any time the couple mentioned healing, Riku would insist he was not like one of "those people."

It can be difficult for Japanese people to admit they struggle with a mental health issue. Many fear being stigmatized. Treatment in Japan often focuses on medication without the support of counseling.

In another troubling trend, suicides of young people climbed to a thirty-year high in 2018[4]—it was the number one cause of death among 15-39 year olds in Japan.[5] The number of school children committing suicide typically peaks after the summer break. There can be several contributing factors to this, including family issues, bullying, and academic pressures.

There is, however, a growing awareness of mental and emotional health issues both in society and the church. Government-funded suicide prevention strategies are showing some success. And more Christians are interested in going into mental health professions.

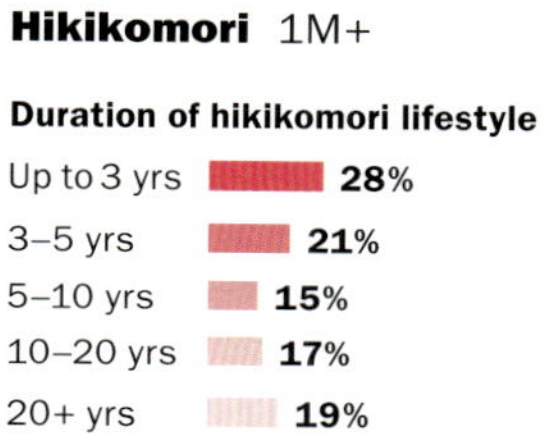

Source: https://bit.ly/2ZgSXIH

Pray that seeking mental health care would lose its current stigma in Japan.

Pray for more Christian counselors, and that the church would be equipped to minister to those who are struggling.

Pray that more Japanese people would discover God's grace and acceptance, and that Christians would model this for them.

9

Aging society

Celeste saw an elderly Japanese man fall out of his wheelchair on the sidewalk and helped him get home. She told him the address of her church, and later that week, he met her there. It was his first time in a church.

In 2020 more than 28% of Japan's population was aged 65 and over.[6] This is thought to be the highest proportion of elderly in any country and is increasing as Japan's population shrinks due to declining birthrates and a growing number of "lifelong singles."

There are enormous long-term implications. Labor shortages have led to increased immigration and investment in artificial intelligence (AI). The healthcare and pension systems are under stress and many are concerned about the future.

A growing number of elderly people live alone and are becoming socially isolated. The number of those dying alone at home has also been increasing. Some districts are making efforts to promote the well-being of senior citizens through campaigns and events.

Christians are also trying to reach out. Some churches run exercise classes or host seniors' lunches. Pastors visit elderly church members who are housebound or in hospitals. There are even elderly Christians who volunteer in nursing homes, seeking to befriend their peers.

Age 65 and over
Highest percentages in the world

Japan	28%
European Union	20%
North America	16%
East Asia & Pacific	11%
World average	9%

Source: https://bit.ly/343XOAi

Give thanks for faithful elderly believers and pray they will share their faith with their peers.

Pray for Japanese churches to minister to the elderly, many of whom are lonely.

Pray for wisdom for the Japanese government and other leaders making decisions about issues such as healthcare, pensions, and community programs.

10

Politics and international relations

Japan's international relations have changed since World War II. Having initially focused on restoring relations with the United States, the Japanese government now tends to follow them. Key issues with Asian neighbors, however, remain unresolved—including relations with North Korea, the disputed Northern Territories, and the use of comfort women and forced labor during the war.

Domestically, the government has enacted a State Secrecy Law and a Conspiracy Law, and there is concern that freedom of press has declined. The sections in the Constitution that renounce war have been re-interpreted to authorize the right to collective self-defense. Priority has been given to improving the economy while environmental and human rights concerns remain.

Separation of state and religion has been preserved in local governments, where spending on Shinto shrines is considered unconstitutional. Yet in 2019, during the enthronement ceremonies of the new emperor, the national government used 2.44 billion yen (22 million USD) of public funds for the *Daijōsai*, the most significant ceremony of Shinto.

Some people are also concerned that patriotic education in Japanese schools, the compulsory use of the national flag and anthem, and visits to significant Shinto shrines by the prime minister and other politicians may indicate the rise of ethnic nationalism.

Pray that the leaders and people of Japan would humbly use their influence in the world for good.

Pray that the principles of freedom of belief and separation of state and religion would be preserved.

Pray that Japan and its Asian neighbors would be able to find peaceful resolution to their disputes.

11

Immigration and foreign nationals

When Hoa reached the cash register at the convenience store, she noticed that the employee's nametag had the same last name as hers.

"Are you from Vietnam?" she asked in Vietnamese.

"Yes! Are you?"

They found out that they were studying at the same university and decided to meet for lunch that week.

The influx of foreign nationals into Japan has steadily increased in recent years and is expected to continue. Many come as professionals, skilled workers, or students. Others come as spouses. In 2019 the government made a significant policy change to bring in workers for industries such as manufacturing, agriculture, and nursing care to help meet critical labor shortages.

As a mainly homogenous society that values conformity, Japan faces numerous challenges integrating new people. Foreign nationals also face challenges. They need to adjust to the culture, working environment, and high cost of living in Japan, as well as learn the language.

Some of the foreign nationals are missionaries on religious visas. Other Christians have intentionally found secular jobs in Japan and are building relationships in their workplaces. Churches are being planted among diaspora groups like Filipinos, Brazilians, and Chinese, and several cities now have multi-ethnic international churches.

Pray for Japanese officials and organizations as they oversee the influx of foreign nationals.

Pray for Christian foreign nationals to be a blessing to their Japanese neighbors in schools, workplaces, and communities.

Pray that Japanese churches will reach out to foreign nationals and partner with diaspora groups and ethnic churches.

12

Natural disasters

On March 11, 2011, the largest recorded earthquake in Japan struck the region of Tohoku, triggering a massive tsunami and nuclear reactor failure. Known as *3.11*, this sparked Japan's worst humanitarian crisis since World War II. But this is not Japan's only disaster in recent years. The country continues to be hit by typhoons, earthquakes, and flooding.

Before *3.11*, most Christian relief work in Japan was ad hoc. This led to an unequal distribution of volunteers based on relationship rather than need. Since then local church networks have been formed, which allow aid to reach communities more evenly.

Disaster response has become an important part of Christian ministry in Japan. There has been a visible improvement of Christian witness in areas that were resistant to the gospel. This has resulted in new believers, churches planted, and more long-term Christian workers.

The Japanese government's preparedness for and response to natural disasters is among the best in the world. It is effective in providing supplies, recovering victims, and making repairs. However, most disaster survivors need ongoing help as they struggle to cope with the losses they have suffered. The church can walk alongside them in the love and hope of Christ.

Pray for church networks to be strengthened and new ones to be started, so that relief efforts can reach communities effectively.

Pray for chaplains and churches to be trained to provide emotional care to survivors and minister to them well.

Pray for more long-term Christian workers to live and minister in rural areas hit by disasters.

13

Technology and media

For more than five decades Japan has had an international reputation for cutting-edge technology. Visitors expect to see multilingual robots in stores, to be immersed in sophisticated virtual reality games, and to ride on the *shinkansen* (bullet train). Technology and media impact every sphere of society in Japan, including the church.

Some progress has been made in producing Christian apps for children and adults, including one of the Japanese Bible. Social media and digital content are being used to share the gospel and to encourage believers, especially those who are isolated or live a long way from a church. But many Japanese churches with elderly congregations are struggling to keep up, as was evident during the COVID-19 pandemic. Churches without the capacity to move Sunday services online turned to mailing paper copies or CD recordings of sermons to congregants.

There are of course downsides to technology and media. We see young and old fixated on their phones, connected with content but disconnected from people. Some find their fullest identity and relationships in virtual settings rather than in their offline lives. The internet has created a platform for cybercrimes, pornography, bullying, and online predators. Concerns about privacy and false content continue to increase.

Pray that Japanese Christian content creators, social media influencers, and tech developers will use online platforms to share the gospel and strengthen believers.

Pray that Japanese people's hearts would turn to God and away from the evils that are aided by technology, like pornography.

Pray that Japanese Christians would be examples of healthy engagement with technology and media.

14

Workplace pressure

Many Japanese workplaces exert relentless pressure on their workers. Permanent employees are often expected to work long hours and put the company before family and personal life.

One foreigner said: "When I first came to Japan, I was shocked that the father of my host family almost never saw his two small boys during the week and had little energy to engage with them on weekends."

This pressurized lifestyle can adversely affect mental and emotional health, and even be a cause of suicide or death by overwork (*karoshi*).

Casual workers may be able to work fewer hours, but their pay often only covers basic living costs, and they don't receive the same benefits as permanent employees.

Sundays may be the only day people have to recuperate from a tiring week. For Christians, attending church on their only day off can feel like just another thing to do. Non-Christians who are interested in the gospel may simply not have the time or energy to take the next steps.

Thankfully, there are signs that the work culture may be gradually changing. Many in the younger generation are seeking a better work/life balance and the government is introducing some new initiatives.

Pray for government and company leaders to prioritize the importance of taking care of their workers.

Pray that non-Christians interested in the gospel would have the opportunity and energy to pursue Christ.

Pray for Christians to have wisdom to balance the demands of work with family, church, and rest.

4F
3F
東急プラザ
King of
Beef

15

Family life

"All my father cares about is work, so I'm doing whatever I want. He thinks I'm in California to study, but I'm here for the girls and the drugs."

This young Japanese man didn't know that the missionary he was sitting next to on the plane had counseled his father only weeks earlier.

The father had said, "I've been a slave to my work and neglected my family. Now my son won't talk to me unless he wants money. How can I get him back?"

The missionary had explained the parable of the prodigal son to the father. On the plane he shared it with the son. Today father and son are reconciled and attend church together.

The daily average time Japanese fathers spend with their children is measured in minutes. They don't see much of their wives either. Disconnectedness, loneliness, and confusion within families is widespread. Young people are avoiding marriage in increasing numbers. The government views low birth rates as a national crisis.

This situation has led some to seek the true meaning of marriage, help with parenting, or support for struggling children. Addressing family issues has provided opportunities to introduce biblical truths.

Pray that churches will minister to their communities through addressing family issues and lead many families to faith.

Pray that helpful, good quality Christian resources on family life will be produced in Japanese.

Pray that more families would come to Christ, and for the lives of Christian families to attract others to Jesus.

16

Youth and young adults

"I feel like I'm just no good at being a Christian. I hardly read the Bible on my own, and even when I do, I don't get it," Hiroko confided to a staff member. It was 2 a.m. at a KGK* camp for university students. After a day of fellowship and fun, Hiroko poured out her heart.

"When I pray, I feel like I'm just talking to myself. I sometimes wonder if God even exists. I have a hard time wanting to go to church. I'm the only one my age there. Sometimes I just want to give up."

Unfortunately, Hiroko's struggles are not uncommon in Japan. Christians are a tiny minority, and many churches are small and aging with few, if any, young people.

Young people in Japan, both Christian and non-Christian, may struggle with a number of concerns—among them, academic pressures, family, relationships, and their futures. It's difficult to transition from university to the workplace, and concerns about finances have made young adults reluctant to get married or have children.

It is vital for Christian young people to find fellowship and be equipped to share their faith with their peers. Parachurch organizations like KGK play a key role.

*KGK is a campus ministry, like InterVarsity in the US. It is affiliated with the International Fellowship of Evangelical Students (IFES).

Give thanks for Christian organizations like KGK, hi-b.a. (for high schoolers), and others that minister to Japanese young people.

Pray for believers who will care for and mentor young people in their Christian walk.

Pray that Japanese Christian youth would have joy in their faith and courage to share it with others.

17

Struggling churches

Jeff and Sandra came to serve at a church whose former pastor had burned out. They quickly discovered that church members depended solely on the leader to keep them fed spiritually. The former pastor also thought that was his calling and had not challenged those ideas. Over the next five years, as church members engaged with God's Word themselves, they learned to work together in building up the church.

Many struggling churches have a common feature: the pastor leads and members attend or participate minimally. One reason is cultural. The pastor is a teacher in the church. In Japanese culture, it's appropriate to follow and submit to a teacher, rather than to walk alongside.

Another reason is the busyness of church members. Schools and companies hold events on Sundays and attendance is often compulsory. On weeks without events, Sunday might be their only day off. Some are simply too tired to attend church, let alone serve or engage with others.

Churches can start to lack joy, fellowship, and ownership. This can lead to a lack of outreach and few new believers. On top of cultural and social factors, churches face a very real spiritual battle and it is easy to get discouraged.

Pray for believers to be willing and able to use their gifts to build up the church and reach out to their communities.

Pray for God to strengthen members and leaders through worship, the Word, and fellowship.

Pray for churches to understand their challenges and receive God's grace to overcome them

18

Church planting

For a detailed map of unchurched areas in Japan, see https://bit.ly/3IR4I2r.

Many Christian leaders are dreaming that God would multiply his church in Japan so that everyone has easy access to a church—one for every community. That would mean more than 50,000 churches. There were fewer than 8,000 Protestant churches in 2016.[7]

Japanese people are the world's second largest unreached people group.[8] One of the primary strategies for evangelizing people groups is planting churches that reproduce to plant more churches. But many places still need their first church.

Challenges include limited numbers of leaders and resources, and overwhelming needs within existing churches. Church planting cannot easily be done alone, but many pastors struggle to find like-minded lay people to join them or to commit to outreach. They also need networks that can support them through the difficult initial stages.

But there are some encouraging examples of church planting movements. The Japan Church Growth Institute has helped set up about 30 church planting networks across Japan. This has led to more than 160 new churches since 1996.[9] Another network in Tokyo started with one church in 2010 and grew to ten within the decade.

Pray for God to saturate Japan with vibrant churches so that every Japanese person can access a Christian community.

Pray for a new generation of church planters that includes pastors, missionaries, and lay leaders.

Pray that Japanese churches would work together to encourage church planting movements in their areas.

19

Church leadership

Pastor Yamanaka has a passionate desire to shepherd his church. He longs to equip members to live out the good news in their neighborhoods, workplaces, and schools. However, his church faces various challenges, and being in his mid-seventies, Pastor Yamanaka also needs to find someone to replace him.

There is great concern about the future of church leadership in Japan. In 2016 nearly half of the pastors in Japan were over the age of seventy. Only 10 percent were under fifty years old. One in eight churches had no pastor[10] and seminaries reported decreasing enrollments.

Pastor Kimura is a recent seminary graduate in his thirties who oversees two churches. He wants to be mentored as a Christian leader, but struggles to find time for this. He would like to stay in touch with seminary friends for mutual support, but they are busy too.

Japanese pastors have tremendous ministry responsibilities and a limited support team, if any at all. Japan has a great need for young pastors who will faithfully preach God's Word and shepherd his people. But as they are called, young pastors must also be supported and encouraged, so that they can continue in ministry for the years ahead.

Age of pastors

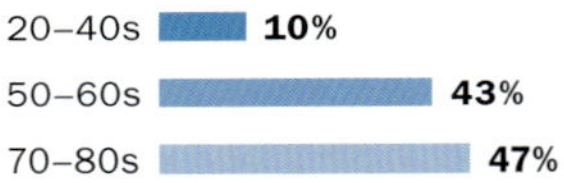

Pray for older pastors to trust and equip the next generation for leadership and evangelism.

Pray for God to give daily refreshing and strength to Japanese pastors, both young and old.

Pray for many Japanese believers to be called by God into pastoral ministry and to have the support they need to thrive in it.

20

Church in the community

"Can I have more ice cream?" The petite five-year-old girl had already eaten two bowlfuls. It was her first meal of the day. Her mother had sent her three daughters out of the house that morning when her new boyfriend came to visit. Later that day, the three girls had shown up at the church's summer neighborhood event.

Single parent families often struggle to make ends meet. Homeless people sleep in subway stations or under bridges. One in seven children live below Japan's poverty line.[11] Despite Japan's reputation as a wealthy nation, poor and marginalized people can be found throughout the country.

It can seem easier to reach out to those whose struggles are visible. The majority of people in Japan—the middle class and the rich—can look like they have everything they need. But that is not always the case; they may have hidden emotional or other needs. It is only through authentic relationships that we discover what people are really searching for.

The church the little girl had shown up at was within walking distance of two elementary schools. This is why they held children's events. Other churches have different opportunities to make genuine connections with the communities around them.

Give thanks for churches that are actively seeking to meet the needs of their communities.

Pray that church members would develop genuine relationships with people in their communities.

Pray that the church would be a place where people from all parts of society experience Christ's presence.

21

Creative ways of ministry

Opposite a local subway station is a small café—seven tables around a long one in the middle of the room. It's where a retired quantum mechanics professor connects with a younger autistic man and where patients from a nearby mental health clinic come with their therapist for lunch. Others come to find community. This café is a ministry run by missionaries to reach people through authentic connections.

This kind of ministry is one creative way to reach out to communities in Japan. Some churches reach out through kids' programs, English clubs, or hobby groups like quilting or cycling. Other churches have contemporary worship or bilingual services that appeal to younger people.

Christians in Japan are using sports, social media, music, and more to creatively engage people who are unlikely to enter a church building. A snowboarder shares about Christ on the ski lift. A Japanese pastor does the same on his surfboard. A Japanese church starts a monthly board-game night. A missionary couple shares original Christian songs at open mic events.

There are people of all backgrounds and interests in Japan. Creativity and wisdom are needed to enter into their lives and share Christ in authentic ways.

Give thanks for creative ways of ministry in Japan, and pray for more.

Pray that churches can find authentic ways to connect with different groups in Japanese society.

Pray that Christian workers can find ways to partner with others and not burn out amidst the vast opportunities.

22

Christianity in rural areas

In the rural north of Japan's main island, Nozomi was working at a clothing store in the area's only shopping mall. There she met church planters who invited her to a dessert party. This led to a Thanksgiving event, a Christmas service, a Bible study, and finally Nozomi's declaration of faith. She later became the manager of the prefecture's only Christian bookstore.

In Japan, the concept of "rural" includes less densely populated cities of regional significance, as well as smaller towns and villages. A bleak picture is often painted of these areas. The youth are moving away to big cities. Churches are aging and many are without pastors. Residents like to preserve traditional ways, and it is easy to assume that hearts are closed to the gospel.

Regional governments are trying to revitalize some rural areas—building roads and promoting tourism. As a result, small regional cities are now more accessible, and new relationships may be easier to make there than in Japan's megacities.

More than 40 million Japanese people live in these areas.[12] Christ's teachings are attractive to them, but the work can be slow. Long-term Christian workers are needed to live out and share the gospel.

Pray for more Christian workers to commit long-term to reach the tens of millions who live in rural areas.

Pray that the Holy Spirit would draw those living in rural Japan to Christ as they hear the gospel.

Pray for wisdom for regional governments as they make decisions about local challenges.

23

Personal evangelism

Joe, a missionary, and two short-term workers were on a tour. They entered a Buddhist temple and saw statues representing the twelve Chinese zodiac creatures on a table. The guide asked them what year they were born.

When one of the short-termers discovered she was born in the year of the sheep, she said, "That's fitting. I am a sheep and Jesus is my good shepherd."

The guide, Tomoko, didn't understand, so Joe explained the biblical reference. Tomoko listened intently and at the end of the tour, she asked to become Joe's Facebook friend. She often engages with his posts.

On another occasion, a Japanese believer said to Joe's wife, "I wish I could talk with non-believers like your husband does."

Japanese values, including group harmony and not bothering others, can make it difficult for Japanese people to identify as Christians and initiate conversations about Jesus. This is especially true with people they see often, like neighbors, classmates, or coworkers.

Other times, when it comes to sharing their faith, believers may worry that they don't know enough about God or the Bible, and that they might say the wrong thing. But many desire to be greater witnesses where they live and work.

Pray that Japanese Christians would joyfully share their personal lives and testimonies with those around them.

Pray that Christians would intentionally go out to meet people and share the gospel in word and deed.

Pray that the Holy Spirit would work in the hearts of Japanese non-believers every time they interact with Christians.

24

Faith in the workplace

While waiting to board a packed Tokyo-bound train, a salaryman engaged Mark, a missionary, in conversation. The man apologized profusely that he was drunk—he was on his way to visit the grave of his recently deceased sister and had been drinking with his coworkers. He then poured out his heart, in public, to a total stranger.

This man, like many in Japan, was in need of a place to be heard and belong (an *ibasho*). Mark asked if he could pray for him; the salaryman nodded and listened.

The workplace may seem like the easiest setting to reach out to working people. But harmonious relationships with coworkers is key in Japan, and many Japanese Christians struggle to express their faith at work because of the pressure not to stand out. On top of that, Christians can feel stretched by their responsibilities and the demands of their bosses.

There may be few Christians in any given workplace, often only one, so they can feel isolated or timid. But with each believer, there is an opportunity for someone at the next desk or across the aisle to hear about and receive the *ibasho* we have in Christ.

Pray that Japanese Christians would have the courage to be open about their faith at work.

Pray that Christians would see their work as an important way they can serve God in the world and be a light to their coworkers.

Pray that Christians in positions of influence would impact their workplace culture and values in godly ways.

25

Daily Christian life and faith

Ayako became a Christian at university. Her mother was adamantly opposed to her baptism, but Ayako remained strong in her faith.

After graduating, Ayako shared with her missionary friend Sun-young that she was struggling. Her veterinary job was stressful, and she had little peace at home with her mother.

Ayako asked, "I feel like my life with Jesus is separate from my working life. How can I bring them together?"

In Japanese culture, keeping private and public lives separate is highly valued, and religion is often reserved for special occasions or times of need. Christians may attend church on Sundays, but have difficulty discussing their faith over lunch with a non-Christian coworker.

There is also a clear hierarchy between teachers and students or *senpai* and *kohai* (seniors and juniors). This is seen in schools, clubs, and companies. In churches, many Christians think it is best to learn the Bible through a pastor or missionary. They may struggle to study the Bible on their own during the week.

Ayako and Sun-young talked about praying in the ordinary places and routines of life. Ayako could pray silently on the subway, ask God for wisdom while working, or even pray in the bath.

Pray for those who struggle with their faith in the midst of busy lives or family opposition.

Pray for Christians to find creative ways to bring the Bible and prayer into their regular routines.

Pray that they will know how to apply biblical values and principles to their situations and relationships.

サマリヤの女との対話
イエスがヨハネよりも多く弟子をつくって、バプ
テスマを授けているということが、パリサイ人の耳にはいっ

26

Japanese overseas

Rina had been a seeker at a church in Tokyo before she went to study in London. The pastor was later delighted to hear that she had come to faith while overseas.

In 2019 more than 1.3 million Japanese were living abroad. It is estimated that every year nearly 1,000 Japanese people become Christians overseas.[13]

This is a high percentage compared to those living in Japan, but as one church plant in Tokyo experienced, it can work the other way too. Some members became seekers overseas and then came to faith in Japan. God had been planting seeds in places as far-flung as Australia, Boston, and Singapore.

Living abroad presents many challenges—language, a new culture, and distance from family and friends. Churches and Christian home-stay families around the world have an amazing opportunity to welcome Japanese people and share the gospel with them.

Coming back to Japan can also be difficult. Seekers or new believers may feel discouraged if friends and family don't understand the changes they are going through. They may struggle to find a church or other Christians nearby. Finding a caring community can help them replant and grow.

*Returnees are those who move overseas, often to study or work, then "return" to their home country.

Pray for churches and ministries outside Japan as they seek to reach out to Japanese people.

Pray that Japanese people living overseas would be open to the gospel and meet believers who can lead them to Christ.

Pray that returnees* would find church communities in Japan that will love and support them.

27

Missionary life

Jack arrived in Japan as a new missionary. He was fired up—ready to learn Japanese and get out there to make a difference. His mission agency required him to attend a local Japanese church, but he soon became worn out. He thought, "What's the point of going if I don't know what they're saying and can't talk to anyone?"

After a few months, he realized that he still struggled to order a meal and certainly wasn't able to explain the gospel in Japanese yet. Amidst the difficulties, Jack began to lose sight of why he was in Japan.

New missionaries need to persevere and maintain their spiritual fervor, especially when they understand little of the language and culture. Families have the added stress of helping their children adjust. Missionaries may face cultural stress working with teammates from different countries. They can also feel pressure to appear as though they are coping, and not admit their struggles. Seasoned missionaries are not exempt and can be discouraged by a lack of fruit.

But missionaries also have testimonies of thankfulness and joy because they've experienced God sustaining them through challenges. They know his ongoing call in their lives and see him at work in and through them.

Pray that missionaries would persevere in learning Japanese language and culture to communicate the gospel more effectively.

Pray for missionaries to be mindful of how they are doing spiritually, physically, and emotionally so they can continue long term.

Pray against discouragement, a common weapon of the enemy against missions work in Japan.

28

Unity in Christ

A retired missionary shared a story about a church plant in northern Tokyo. A cult had swept through the region in 1952, scaring people away, and the church had hit a low with zero attendance one Sunday. So the team began to meet daily to pray for revival. Their biggest challenge was unity between teammates, but they persevered and came to a place of oneness and respect.

After months of prayer, 40 people came to hear an evangelist the team had barely advertised. Following a message on how the Holy Spirit brings repentance, most stayed until midnight, heads bent, confessing their sin.

Another missionary shared about a prefecture that was known in the 1970s for disunity among the churches. In the mid-90s there was a movement among pastors that started with an annual four-day prayer summit. These led to monthly half-day prayer meetings. Since then there has been reconciliation and a change in the spiritual climate. Churches from all over the prefecture now gather for an annual day of praise and worship.

Christians in Japan face many challenges to the spread of the gospel. But in unity, we gain strength and glorify God. May God give churches, mission organizations, and believers the grace to serve together.

Pray that unity among believers, which leads to reconciliation and revival, would increase in this decade.

Pray that churches and leaders would pray for and encourage each other.

Pray for churches, denominations, and mission organizations to work together to advance the gospel in Japan.

29

Japanese mission movement

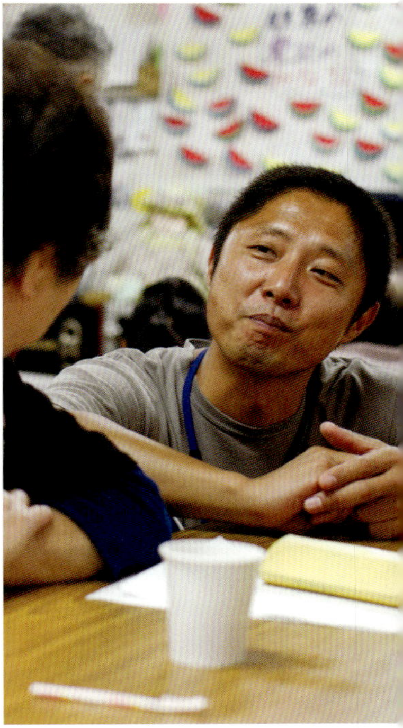

Haruto, a Japanese Bible college student, has sensed God's call to overseas missions for some time. He knows that many Japanese churches lack pastors. Additionally, his denomination expects that Haruto will work at one of their churches after he graduates. These two factors cause him to struggle with the call he feels on his heart.

There are some Japanese churches that faithfully pray for and support overseas missions, but others don't seem to have much interest or capacity. Many churches have financial struggles and/or lack church workers. It can be hard to think beyond the needs of their own church or denomination.

God is raising up young people like Haruto who sense God's call to world mission. However, they face many challenges along the way, such as how to get training and raise financial and prayer support.

There is an urgent need in Japan for biblical teaching about God's desire for his church to reach out to the whole world. Even if they feel small and powerless, we long to see many more Japanese churches take up the responsibility and privilege of God's global mission. This will not only bless many nations, but Japan as well.

Give thanks for Japanese missionaries serving overseas and pray for those who sense God's call to join them.

Pray that Japanese churches will take up the challenge of being involved in God's mission, and find joy in doing so.

Pray for effective mobilization by mission agencies in Japanese churches and Bible colleges.

30

Prayer for spiritual breakthrough

Missionaries who have served long-term in Japan often emphasize the necessity of prayer over any one strategy or ministry philosophy. There has long been a conviction that committed prayer is needed for a significant breakthrough of the gospel in Japan.

There is also a growing global interest in praying for Japan—mission agencies are receiving emails and inquiries from around the world. And social media provides an easy way to share prayer needs.

A conviction to pray, a global body of Christians who want to pray, and the means to share information—these are rich starting materials for a prayer movement.

Believers in Japan long for spiritual breakthrough that will impact the culture, society, and church. Together with believers around the world, we want to chip away at these huge topics with specific, informed prayers.

We also long for breakthrough in every person. We yearn for Japanese believers to be deeply rooted in Christ, new believers to be mentored, and many more to be added to their number.

Spiritual breakthrough requires follow-up by churches and ministries. We ask for God's strength and provision of all that will be needed for the harvesting work to come.

Praise God that he is calling people all over the world to pray for spiritual breakthrough in Japan.

Pray for resources to equip people to pray in informed ways for Japan.

Pray that God would prepare churches and Christians in Japan to respond to a breakthrough of people coming to faith.

References

1 Don Wright, *Operation Japan Prayer Guide*, 5th edition (2019), 10.

2 Roger W. Lowther, *The Broken Leaf: Meditations on Art, Life, and Faith in Japan* (Eugene, Oregon: Wipf & Stock, 2019).

3 Ministry of Internal Affairs and Communications, "Monthly Report," Statistics Bureau of Japan, March 1, 2020, https://bit.ly/3aInsvE.

4 From "2015 Population Census," Ministry of Internal Affairs and Communications. More detail available on request at jp.info@omfmail.com.

5 Eiraku Maiko, "Japan's 'Hikikomori' are growing older," NHK World-Japan, May 6, 2019, https://bit.ly/2FKHg6j.

6 "Child Suicides at Highest Rate Ever in Japan," nippon.com, November 5, 2019, https://bit.ly/3aVsVj3.

7 "Japan the only G-7 country where young people are most likely to die from suicide," *The Mainichi*, July 17, 2019, https://bit.ly/34ghDEB, Japanese original by Takuya Murata.

8 From "Summary Report 2016," Ministry of Health, Labour, Welfare. More detail available on request at jp.info@omfmail.com.

9 データブック日本宣教のこれからが見えてくるーキリスト教の30年後を読む [Databook: Seeing the Future of Mission in Japan—Christianity in 30 years' time] (Japan: Inochi no kotoba sha, 2016), 45.

10 Ibid, 11.

11 "Unreached: 100 Largest," Joshua Project, https://bit.ly/3huwsHz (accessed August 2020).

12 John Wm. Mehn, *Multiplying Churches in Japanese Soil* (Colorado: William Carey Library, 2017), 77.

13 Matthew Cummings, "Welcoming them home," *Japan Harvest*, https://bit.ly/31itLDf (accessed August 2020).

Website

Visit www.japanprayerguide.com for links to order, translations, and more.